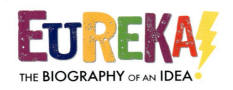

Guitar

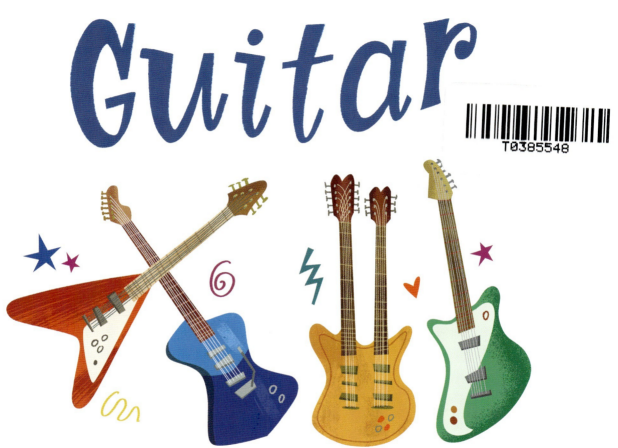

BY LORI HASKINS HOURAN • ILLUSTRATED BY KALY QUARLES

AN IMPRINT OF ASTRA BOOKS FOR YOUNG READERS
New York

For Dad, my favorite guitarist —LHH

For my sweet Ryan, the best in the west! —KQ

Special thanks to Monica Smith, Associate Director, the Smithsonian's Lemelson Center for the Study of Invention and Innovation

Library of Congress Cataloging-in-Publication Data

Names: Houran, Lori Haskins, author. | Quarles, Kaly, illustrator.
Title: Guitar / by Lori Haskins Houran ; illustrated by Kaly Quarles.
Description: First edition. | New York : Kane Press, 2023. | Series: Eureka! | Audience: Ages 4-8 | Audience: Grades K-1 | Summary: "With a timeline spanning from the first time someone strummed a string stretched across a hollow object to electric guitars that bring stadiums of people to their feet today, Guitar is a fun and informative look at the development of an invention that adds music to our lives. This STEAM nonfiction title is part of the Eureka! series, with each book focusing on one groundbreaking, world-changing discovery that millions of people use every single day"—Provided by publisher.
Identifiers: LCCN 2022007705 (print) | LCCN 2022007706 (ebook) | ISBN 9781662670053 (hardcover) | ISBN 9781635928211 (paperback) | ISBN 9781635928228 (epub)
Subjects: LCSH: Guitar—Juvenile literature.
Classification: LCC ML1015.G9 H68 2023 (print) | LCC ML1015.G9 (ebook) | DDC 787.87/19—dc23
LC record available at https://lccn.loc.gov/2022007705
LC ebook record available at https://lccn.loc.gov/2022007706

Kane Press
An imprint of Astra Books for Young Readers,
a division of Astra Publishing House
kanepress.com
Printed in China

10 9 8 7 6 5 4 3 2 1

TURN ON YOUR FAVORITE SONG. It can be any kind of music. Country. Pop. Jazz. Rock. Chances are, you'll hear a guitar.

The story of the guitar starts thousands of years ago.

Someone dried a strip of animal skin to make string. They stretched it over something hollow. A scooped-out gourd, maybe. Or a carved piece of wood.

Then they plucked the string with their fingers, and it made a sound. A very pleasing sound!

This was the first **string instrument** . . . and the first step toward the guitar.

AROUND 3000 BCE

Some of the oldest string instruments we know about came from Mesopotamia, Africa, and Persia.

The **oud** was shaped like a teardrop. Musicians used eagle or peacock feathers to pluck its strings.

Nyatiti players wore a metal ring around their big toe. They banged it on the side of the instrument to keep time while they strummed.

The **tanbur** had a long, skinny neck. It was played with a narrow piece of tortoiseshell.

nyatiti

oud

tanbur

7

700s CE

Around the year 711, soldiers carried ouds with them to Spain.

Spanish craftsmen tinkered with the oud. They made it bigger and added more strings. They also tied loops of string, called **frets**, around its neck. Musicians could press the frets to make different notes.

The instrument got a new name, too—the **lute**.

Lute players performed all over Europe. In pubs, theaters, and even castles! They played for kings and queens at parties . . .

. . . and strummed them to sleep afterward. *Shhhhh!*

800s TO 1500s

The lute stayed popular for centuries. Meanwhile, people created more and more string instruments.

spinet

fiddle

cittern

harp

Some didn't stick around. The Spanish **vihuela** appeared around 1480 . . . and pretty much disappeared by 1580.

But its curvy shape inspired an instrument that *did* last—the guitar!

vihuela

1500s To 1800s

Early guitars were small, around two or three feet long. They were very quiet.

At first, their soft sound was fine. People mostly played these "parlor guitars" at home, by themselves.

But music was changing. Composers started writing songs for musicians to play together in big concert halls.

Guitar players wanted to join in. Only, they kept getting drowned out! The guitar needed to get louder. How?

To figure it out, guitar makers thought hard about the way guitars make sound.

HOW A GUITAR MAKES SOUND

When you strum a guitar's strings, they vibrate.

strings and vibrations

sound waves inside guitar body

The vibrations create sound waves. The waves bounce around inside the guitar's hollow body. The more they bounce, the bigger and louder they get. In other words, the sound waves are **amplified**.

sound hole

Finally, the waves bounce out of the guitar's sound hole . . . and into your ears!

AROUND 1850

In Spain, Antonio de Torres Jurado found one way to make guitars louder. Make them larger! That gave the sound waves more space to bounce around.

He designed a guitar with a long, deep body—almost twice as deep as a parlor guitar. Many guitars built today still follow his design.

Other people wondered—could different strings help, too?

Guitar strings hadn't changed much since ancient times. They were made of **catgut**, which came from dried sheep guts. (Not cat guts, despite the name!)

Guitar makers tried steel strings. These vibrated much harder than catgut strings. That meant a louder sound.

There was just one problem. Steel strings vibrated SO hard, they pulled the guitar apart!

In New York City, a German immigrant named C. F. Martin came up with a solution. He invented a sturdy brace to hold the guitar together. It stopped the steel strings from causing any damage.

Thanks to a new size and new strings, guitars were plenty loud. At least, for a while . . .

1920s To 1930s

In the 1920s, Americans fell in love with dance hall music. The bands that played it were LOUD. Blaring trumpets! Squealing saxophones! Booming trombones! The guitar was drowned out again.

Around the same time, Americans fell in love with something else—electricity. Inventors used it to power all sorts of things, from light bulbs to radios.

Guitar maker George Beauchamp had a great idea. Why not use electricity to boost the guitar's sound?

Beauchamp created the **pickup**, a device that sat on top of the guitar. It used magnets to "pick up" the sound waves the strings made, and turn them into electric currents.

The currents zipped along a cord to an **amplifier**. This "amp" worked a lot like a radio. Beauchamp could turn the guitar's sound up. WAY up!

Guitarists never had to worry about being loud again.

amplifier

pickup

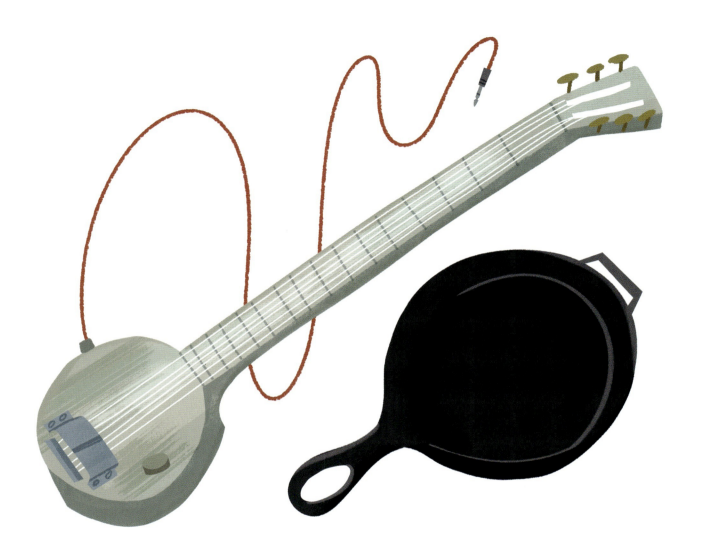

With electricity to amplify the sound, guitars didn't have to be hollow anymore—or even have a sound hole. Beauchamp built a guitar with a solid, round body, nicknamed the Frying Pan. It was the first electric guitar to be sold across the U.S.

1940s TO 1950s

Jazz, country, and blues musicians loved the bold sound of the electric guitar. It even inspired a whole new kind of music. Rock and roll!

The demand for electric guitars soared. Two companies, Fender and Gibson, jumped in to meet it.

In 1951, Fender introduced the Telecaster, a simple solid-body guitar. Gibson mocked it, calling it a cross between a toilet seat and a canoe paddle.

But the Telecaster began to sell. And sell. And sell!

So, Gibson made its own solid-body guitar, the Gibson Les Paul. That took off, too.

Fender shot back with the Stratocaster. It became the most popular electric guitar in the world . . . and still is today!

These days, electric guitars come in all shapes and sizes.
Anything goes!

Of course, not all musicians want electric guitars. Many people prefer **acoustic** guitars—traditional guitars with strings made of steel or nylon. They don't need amps. They're easy to carry. And you can play them just about anywhere.

Whether loud or quiet, electric or acoustic, guitars are a big part of music today.
You wouldn't have your favorite song without them!

••• GUITAR GREATS •••

Here are just a few legendary guitarists.

Sister Rosetta Tharpe played gospel music—but not like anyone had ever heard it! Her rip-roaring style inspired rock-and-roll musicians like Chuck Berry and Elvis Presley.

Blues musician **B.B. King** once ran into a burning building to save his guitar. He gave all his guitars the same nickname: Lucille.

When he was a teenager, **Django Reinhardt** burned two of his fingers. Doctors said he'd never play guitar again. But Reinhardt adapted his style, relying on his other fingers. He became a world-famous jazz guitarist.

For centuries, flamenco guitarists stayed in the background, behind singers and dancers. Then superstar **Ramón Montoya** came along. Fans flocked to hear him play all by himself. No singing or dancing needed!

Many consider **Jimi Hendrix** the greatest guitarist of all time. He could make his guitar wail and howl like no one before him.

Nancy Wilson was the first female guitarist to lead a successful hard rock band, Heart. She played alongside her sister, singer Ann Wilson.

THE PARTS OF A GUITAR

Every guitar has a head, a neck, and a body.

ELECTRIC GUITAR   **ACOUSTIC GUITAR**

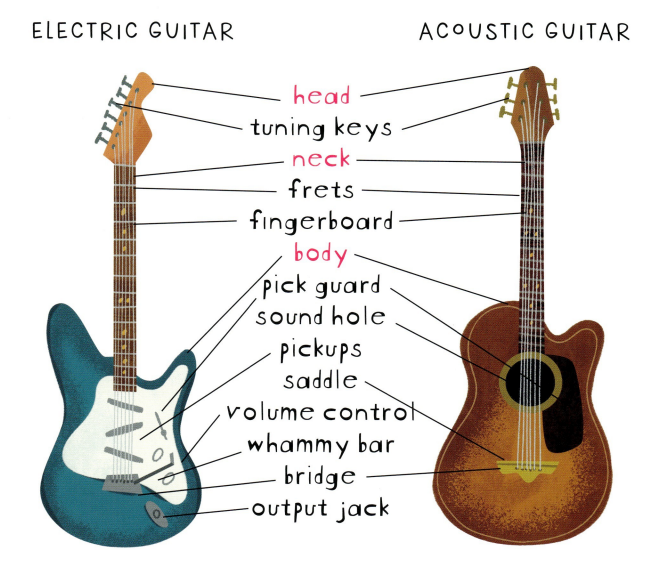

head

tuning keys

neck

frets

fingerboard

body

pick guard

sound hole

pickups

saddle

volume control

whammy bar

bridge

output jack